Kid's Library of Space Exploration

Becoming an Astronaut

Kid's Library of Space Exploration

Kid's Library of Space Exploration

Becoming an Astronaut

Zachary Chastain

VILLAGE EARTH PRESS

Kid's Library of Space Exploration: Becoming an Astronaut

Village Earth Press
Vestal, New York 13850
www.villageearthpress.com

First Printing
9 8 7 6 5 4 3 2 1

Series ISBN (paperback): 978-1-62524-444-4
ISBN (paperback): 978-1-62524-408-6
ebook ISBN: 978-1-62524-043-9

Library of Congress Control Number: 2014931528

Author: Chastain, Zachary.

Contents

ONE

The Early History of Astronauts

The word "astronaut" comes from two Greek words that literally mean "star sailor." Astronauts are the men and women who travel in spaceships into Earth's orbit and beyond. In 1957, humans sent the first object into space—a Russian satellite called *Sputnik*. Then in 1969, the first humans walked on the moon. That's an incredible amount of progress in just over ten years! It wouldn't have happened without the early *pioneers* that opened a new *frontier* for humans.

Yuri Gagarin: First Man in Space

The first human to enter space was a Russian named Yuri Gagarin. Yuri was the third born in

Pioneers are people who go into new places where few people have gone before.

A **frontier** is an unexplored area outside the familiar territory where we live our lives.

Animal Astronauts

In 1957, Russia sent the first dog to space. Her name was Laika. Russian scientists attached nodes to her chest so they could monitor her heartbeat. Laika survived the launch and stayed alive in space for a few days. Sadly, the Russians weren't able to get her spaceship back to earth, so Laika died in orbit. But Laika's mission is still considered a success. It proved that a living creature could survive in space. Shortly after Laika's mission, Russia put the first human into space.

a family of four children. During World War II, the Germans took his two older brothers and sent them to work camps in Poland. A German officer occupied Yuri's family's home, and he and his family were forced to build a clay hut in the backyard, where they lived for over a year. After the war, Yuri's family got their home back and his brothers returned alive from the work camp. This was a very hard time for many Russian families.

Despite these hardships, Yuri was a very good student. He was chosen to attend a special school where he studied tractors. This was a high honor for a Russian student at that time. Going to school to study how to make tractors meant he would have a well-paying job after school. But Yuri had other plans. He joined an airplane club and took flying lessons.

In 1955, Yuri was drafted into the Soviet Air Force. He quickly rose to senior lieutenant—a very high rank—in just two years.

Then, in 1960, Yuri was chosen, along with nineteen other pilots, for the Soviet space program. Soviet leaders decided that they would choose the "first man in space" from this special group of twenty men. They tested each man both physically and mentally, and Yuri stood out from the pack. Even the other *cosmonauts* recognized there was something special about Yuri. In fact, program leaders asked each of the twenty men to choose which man (besides themselves) they thought should be the first Russian in space. All except three chose Yuri.

Before his first spaceflight, doctors examined Yuri and took notes on his personality. They described him as having a "fantastic memory" and a "well-developed imagination." They were looking for a well-rounded person. They needed someone who was not only smart but also creative. No human had ever been to space before, and Soviet scientists didn't know what sort of challenges a cosmonaut would meet in space. They needed someone with a range of skills, someone who could be ready for any situation. (The same is true today. Astronauts need a wide range of skills.) Oh, and one more thing! The Soviets were looking for a short person. Spaceships were still very small, with little room for a passenger. Once again Yuri was the perfect fit: he was 5 feet 2 inches tall.

Valentina Tereshkova: First Woman in Space

Flying had always fascinated Valentina Tereshkova. In 1959, when she was twenty-two, she made her first jump out of an airplane and floated down to Earth on parachute. Valentina didn't know it at the time, but the Soviets had just created a cosmonaut program for women. They were looking for women with experience in skydiving.

In 1961, Valentina and four other skydivers were chosen from a group of four hundred female cosmonauts. At that time, skydiving was an important skill for a cosmonaut to have. The Russians didn't know how to safely land a spacecraft after it reentered the Earth's atmosphere. As the spaceship fell toward Earth, cosmonauts would *eject* from the ship and parachute down to the surface.

Valentina and her fellow cosmonauts trained for months. They completed over a hundred parachute jumps. Finally, Valentina was chosen to fly the first female mission to space. In 1963, she was ready to launch into space aboard her ship, *Vostok 6*.

Russia and the Soviet Union

The Union of Soviet Socialist Republics (also known as the USSR or the Soviet Union for short) consisted of Russia and surrounding countries that today make up Armenia, Azerbaijan, Belarus, Estonia, Georgia, Kazakhstan, Kyrgyzstan, Latvia, Lithuania, Moldova, Tajikistan, Turkmenistan, Ukraine, and Uzbekistan. The USSR was founded in 1922, and it was dissolved in late 1991, leaving Russia on its own, while the other nations that had been part of the USSR now became independent countries.

In Russia, astronauts are called **cosmonauts**. Both are words for people who travel into space.

When you **eject** from a spacecraft or aircraft, you shoot yourself out of it very quickly.

Yuri Gagarin's flight around the Earth was the first time humans had reached outer space. It represented the beginning of an age of exploration, as well as fierce competition between the United States and the Soviet Union.

Valentina Tereshkova (left) was just one of over four hundred applicants for the second trip into space. After her flight, she became very active in Russian politics, and hopes to go into space again one day. She's shown here with NASA astronaut Catherine Coleman.

As Valentina as about to board the rocket ship, she said, "Hey sky, take off your hat, I'm coming!"

After takeoff, her spaceship's computer didn't work properly. It began taking Valentina's ship further and further from Earth, instead of slowly going down toward it! Valentina noticed this and radioed to her command center. With Yuri Gagarin's help, she put new codes into the computer that corrected the spacecraft's direction back toward the Earth. She orbited the Earth for three days before finally returning to land. She ejected, opened her parachute, and landed on a farm in Russia. She hadn't eaten anything for three days. When the owners of the farm asked her to dinner, she disobeyed her orders to return straight to base and accepted their invitation!

Her first flight would also be her last flight. Valentina went on to be a high-level official in the Soviet government and a national celebrity. In 2013, at the age of seventy-six, Valentina offered to take a one-way trip

The first spacewalk was only ten minutes long. The equipment used was not very complicated—just a suit and a rope attached to the spacecraft. Today, astronauts also wear backpacks that work like "jet packs," in case they come detached.

Because there is no air pressure in space, every spacecraft needs a special room called an airlock. This lets astronauts move in and out of the aircraft without the air inside rushing out into space.

to Mars. She pointed out that the mission is very dangerous and it will be difficult to get cosmonauts back to Earth once they land on Mars. But she said that she is willing to go!

Alexei Leonov: First Spacewalk

In 1965, just four years after Yuri Gagarin's famous first flight into space, Alexei Leonov became the first man to walk in space. He floated outside the spacecraft for ten minutes. He controlled his motion by tugging on a 50-foot rope. Alexei almost died during his spacewalk. His space suit started swelling and he almost didn't make it back to his ship in time.

To understand what happened, you need to know a little about air pressure. Air pressure is a concept that is very important to astronaut safety. Although you might not realize it, on Earth the air is constantly

APOLLO 11

CDR

PGA 076

After the problems with Alexei's spacesuit, engineers made sure that future spacesuits were very sturdy and had multiple layers to protect the astronaut. This suit belonged to Neil Armstrong, and was worn during the first moonwalk.

When you're in orbit, you can see the atmosphere of the Earth by looking at the edge of the horizon. It may be invisible to us, but the atmosphere keeps us alive and protects us from the dangers of outer space.

pressing down on you. Air is invisible, of course, but it is not made of nothing. Air is a bunch of molecules like oxygen and carbon dioxide, and it has weight. It pushes down on us all the time, and our bodies are designed to push back. In space, however, there is no air pressure because there's no air (no oxygen or carbon dioxide molecules or anything else). We call these no-pressure zones "vacuums." That's why spacesuits must be sealed tight. Inside a spacesuit, the pressure is set to be like the pressure on Earth. Things under high pressure move to low-pressure areas. If a spacesuit has a leak, then the air inside the high-pressure suit wants to get out of the suit—and that makes the suit puff up. This is what happened to Alexei.

As you can imagine, it was a scary moment when Alexei's spacesuit started inflating. If he lost too much air in his suit he could die from the change in pressure. So he tugged himself back toward the ship as quickly as possible. There he met another problem: his puffed-up suit

Alan Shepard's ship didn't manage to get into orbit, but his short trip to space taught NASA's scientists a lot about how to improve their spacecraft.

was too big to fit through the *airlock*! Alexei was forced to release air from his suit in order to shrink it. This was a dangerous move, causing the pressure to drop inside his suit. But it worked. Alexei squeezed inside before the low pressure made him sick.

Alan Shepard: First American in Space

Alan Shepard is the second person and first American to enter space. His ship entered space on May 5, 1961, only a month after Yuri Gagarin's flight. Alan's ship, the *Freedom 7*, launched into space for only fifteen minutes and never entered orbit. Parachutes attached directly to Alan's spaceship. These heavy-duty parachutes carried the *Freedom 7* safely to the Atlantic Ocean. Alan floated there for eleven minutes before a helicopter lifted him from his ship. The whole mission took less than half an hour.

Did You Know?

Astronauts need to go to the bathroom, just like everyone does. After three hours of waiting on the launch pad, Alan Shepard just couldn't hold it any longer. He managed to turn off the power to his spacesuit before he did his business. He didn't want to damage the suit or, worse, electrocute himself. These days, astronauts wear special underwear that absorbs urine. These high-tech diapers can absorb 1,000 times their own weight in water!

An **airlock** is a special room with controlled pressure and two doors, so that a person can move between areas that have different pressures.

Find Out Even More

Most students use the Internet for their research. One of the best things about the Internet is how quick and easy it is to get information. With just a few clicks you find out how much Alan Shepard's spaceship weighed or find a photograph that shows you what Valentina Tereshkova looks like. The Internet is a powerful tool for learning more about the world.

But the same qualities that make the Internet great—speed and ease of access—also make it difficult to use effectively. It's important to *stay focused* when you do Internet research. Otherwise, you'll never find the information you want.

Start by logging off your chat, Facebook, or email. If you have a phone, think about turning it off. This cuts down on outside distractions. You don't want little bells, whistles and blinking lights while you try to focus on your research.

The next thing you should do is minimize how many "tabs" you open on your browser. A few clicks can take you far from your topic. If you start opening too many tabs, you'll soon find yourself far from your original question. You might feel like you're getting closer to an answer, but chances are good that you're only getting further away.

Make sure to take breaks. Taking a ten-minute break from the computer every hour works well for most people. Use that time to move around and stretch. Sitting in front of the computer for too long makes it harder to stay focused.

TWO

Getting Picked to Be an Astronaut

n 1959, America's National Aeronautics and Space Administration (NASA) began looking for seven men to become the first American astronauts. Before anything else was considered, each man had to meet the following requirements:

- He could not be taller than 5 feet 11 inches and could weigh no more than 180 pounds.
- He had to be less than forty years old and have a college degree.
- And most important of all, he had to have at least 1,500 hours of flying time in jet planes.

In the 1950s, jet planes were still a rare technology. Most pilots flew in planes powered by propellers, and not many pilots had experience with jets.

Jet planes work differently from propeller planes. Jets suck air into cylinders. Inside the cylinder, the air is mixed with fuel and lit on fire.

21

While a rocket is launching, the people inside are under very powerful forces. Today, it is standard procedure for them to wear their spacesuits during the launch, in case anything goes wrong and they are unable to breathe.

The explosion creates a push that shoves the plane through the air. Jet planes can fly higher and go faster than planes with propellers. Flying in a jet is sort of like flying in a rocket, because a pilot experiences some of the same extreme forces. We call this "g-force" (gravity force) because it feels like weight pushing against the pilot or astronaut.

G-Force

Both a jet and a rocket accelerate very quickly. Acceleration measures how quickly an object changes its speed. For instance, a racecar can go from 0 to 190 miles (305 km) per hour in about nine seconds. A jet plane can accelerate even faster than that. When a person is inside an object that accelerates that quickly, she experiences a lot of g-force on her body. The faster an object accelerates, the more weight that person feels against her body. Think about the last time you were in a fast car at a stoplight. If the driver hit the gas pedal hard, you probably felt your body pushed back into the seat. Multiply that feeling by a hundred, and that's how an astronaut feels when her rocket launches!

The First Men in Space

NASA wanted to open the selection process to all Americans, men and women, because they wanted to get the very best talent. But the president at the time, Dwight D. Eisenhower, insisted that all astronauts should be experienced military pilots. At that time in history, no women were allowed in the military, and so no women were allowed yet to apply to be astronauts.

More than five hundred male jet pilots applied for the group, which would be called the Mercury Seven. NASA gave the men difficult mental and physical tests. The men had to run for hours on treadmills. They had to put their feet in ice water for long stretches of time. They had to swim in heavy spacesuits with sneakers on. They had to sit in a room with temperatures around 130° Fahrenheit (54° C). After all the tests were completed, only eighteen men remained. The others had dropped out or been kicked out. From these remaining eighteen, the

The black tiles on the space shuttles helped protect them from the atmosphere's heat during reentry. These tiles needed to be replaced frequently to make sure they didn't fail.

Earth isn't the only planet with an atmosphere that ships need to protect themselves from. The gold disk on the bottom of this image is the heat shield that protected the Curiosity rover as it landed on Mars in 2013.

final seven were chosen. Each man was in great physical shape and each had a genius-level IQ. They were very talented individuals.

Physical fitness and flight experience was so important to NASA because the early missions were tough on an astronaut's body. When re-entering the Earth's atmosphere, an astronaut experiences a lot of force on his body.

You see, the atmosphere is made of gases that surround the Earth like a shield. These gases are thick and protective, and when you pass through them, you create a lot of heat. In order to stay in orbit, spaceships are travelling incredibly fast, and the best way for them to slow down enough to land is to slam them into the Earth's atmosphere. As an object speeds through the atmosphere, it compresses the gases ahead of it, which makes them get very hot. With the right equipment, a spaceship can pass through without burning up, but the process shakes and rattles the ship. When flying at high speeds, a jet pilot experiences similar

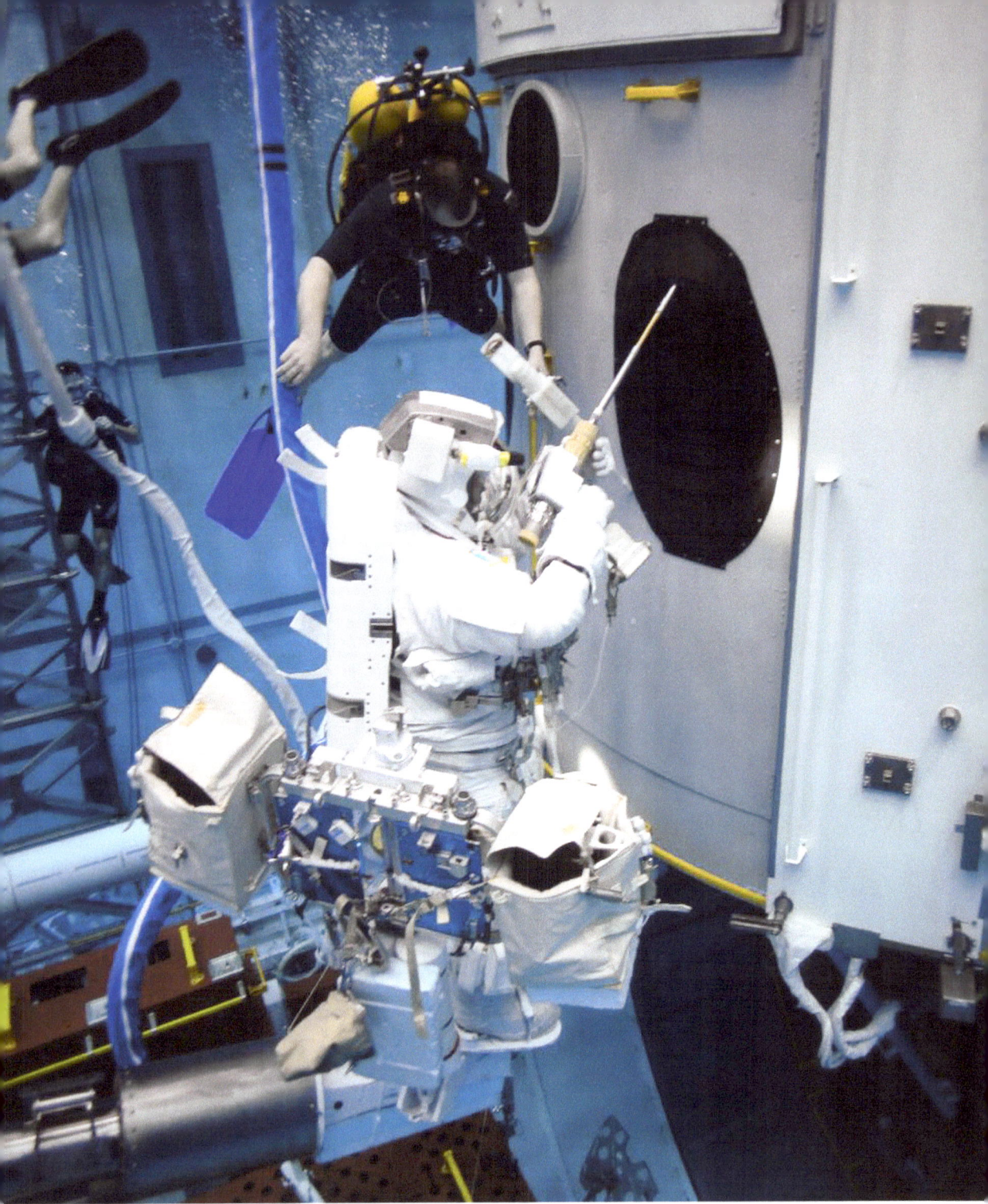

Although many astronauts still begin their careers in the military, NASA is interested in having more and more scientists and teachers go to space. Regardless of where they start, all astronauts must undergo the same intense training. Here, astronauts train underwater, which simulates what it's like to work in zero gravity.

BECOMING AN ASTRONAUT

forces. He must hold onto his controls as his plane powers through the air. It's hard physical work, and it takes a lot of strength.

Over time, the standards for astronauts began to change. Early space flights were like flying a plane on a dangerous mission through clouds and rough storms. The main goal was to get the plane in the air, keep the crew safe, and land safely again in a new location. For those missions, NASA needed astronauts who could handle the extreme physical demands of space travel. But missions began to last longer and give astronauts more time in orbit. Once in orbit, an astronaut could take photos and run tests and experiments. A new astronaut needed not only flight experience but also an ability to study his surroundings.

NASA continued to *recruit* astronauts with military flight experience. But they also began looking for men and women with advanced college degrees. They wanted to send scientists into space, people who could tell us more about what they found there.

Becoming an Astronaut Today

Today, there's more *competition* than ever to become an astronaut. Each year, NASA accepts applications for its training program. If you're one of the lucky people selected, there's no guarantee that you'll become an astronaut, though. Selection only means that you'll begin the astronaut training program at Johnson Space Center in Houston, Texas. In 2013, over 6,100 people applied for the astronaut training program. Only eight people were accepted—and not all of them will ever make it to space.

Today's astronauts must have either lots of experience flying jets, lots of education, or both. After graduating from her first four years of college, an astronaut must have a thousand hours of experience flying a jet or three years of extra education. Those three years can be spent working for a company, but most astronauts spend those years getting more education. Many astronauts have PhD (doctorate) degrees

When you **recruit** people, you hire them or you convince them to work for you.

Competition is when many people want the same thing and are trying to beat each other to get it.

NASA's Jet Propulsion Laboratory, or JPL, is where a lot of the science and development takes place that lets space missions happen. Astronaut candidates with science or engineering experience might end up working here!

from universities. These are the highest degree of education you can get in a subject. Astronauts usually study subjects related to science, math, or engineering. Right now these are the subjects that are thought to be most useful in space.

Candidates are people who are suitable for something, but haven't been picked yet.

Like the first men in space, today's astronauts must be in very good physical health. They must have good eyesight, low blood pressure, and be between 62 and 75 inches tall. That means they must be taller than 5 feet 2 inches and shorter than 6 feet 3 inches. But today, they don't have to be men! Women are also astronauts.

Once selected, a person becomes an official Astronaut Candidate. The 2013 Astronaut Class included four men and four women. Five of the *candidates* had served in the military, and all of them have higher-education degrees. They were all between thirty and forty years of age, and two of them were medical doctors.

Many people do not make the cut. Some of them are offered jobs by NASA, just not as astronauts. These men and women build, design, and plan space missions. They communicate with astronauts from Earth. They design the tools that astronauts take with them to space. That's important work too!

Find Out Even More

One of the main places you'll do your research is on the Internet. That's fine, but believe it or not it's probably not where you should *start* your research. One of your best sources of information is right in your school: your teacher! And if your teacher isn't available, visit your librarian. Let him know what your project is about and what you're looking for. Many times your school will have paid money to receive magazines and get access to online journals or websites. These special sources can give you information you wouldn't get through a regular Internet search.

Your school library is full of resources. If you ask for help, you may avoid hours of Internet research that gets you nowhere. Try thinking of Internet research as an additional tool, not your *only* tool for researching a topic. Start by searching for books in the library's catalog system. Your school library probably has its catalog on a computer. Enter the author, subject, title or keyword into the database, and it will bring up a list of books. Again, if you find the catalog confusing, just ask your librarian for help!

Once you choose a few books that look helpful, write them down on a card. Then ask your librarian to help you find where those books are located. Once you get more confident, you can start finding books without your librarian's help. You do this by using your book's "call number." For example, if your book's call number is 372.23, go the part of the library that's marked "300s." Each section will hold a category of the 300s, such as 300–314, 315–330, and so on. In this case, you'd go to the shelf marked "370–374."

So before you try your favorite search engine, try asking a real person for direction. You may be surprised how much time that can save you!

THREE

Training to Go to Space

So let's say you're one of the eight Astronaut Candidates chosen by NASA in 2013. Now the real work starts. NASA astronauts are trained at the Johnson Space Center in Houston, Texas. The training program usually lasts about two years and involves some skills and activities that you might not expect you'd need for space. Like swimming!

Water Training

Physical fitness is a key part of astronaut training, of course, but swimming is particularly important. Candidates must pass a very difficult swimming test during their first month of training. They must swim three lengths of a pool without stopping. Then they must swim the same distance wearing a flight suit and tennis shoes. Finally, they must tread water for ten minutes without stopping while wearing a flight suit. Why is swimming such an important skill for astronauts? Because when they

In 2011, NASA's space shuttles were retired. After that, most of the trips up to the International Space Station were done using Russian Soyuz spacecraft like this one. Since Russia plays such an important role in the world's space exploration, it's important that NASA's astronauts be able to speak their language!

come back to Earth, the best place for a spaceship to land is the ocean. The astronauts' lives may depend on their being able to swim well.

But there's another reason why astronauts train in water. Water is the perfect place to practice skills for space because it mimics the conditions of weightlessness. There is little or no gravity in space, so there's nothing to tug an astronaut down, which makes her feel weightless. As with air pressure, the human body is built for gravity. When gravity is removed, odd things can happen to the human body. An astronaut who spends too much time without gravity can lose muscle mass and feel sick to her stomach.

When humans float under water, they experience a condition that resembles zero gravity. This is how NASA trains its candidates for space. Astronaut Candidates must pass scuba tests before training for spacewalks. Scuba diving is when people strap on tanks of oxygen and masks so that they can breathe underwater for long periods of time.

Astronaut Skills

These days, astronauts from many different countries must work together. That means that a big part of astronaut training involves learning another language. At the moment, NASA astronauts must travel aboard Russian rockets to reach the International Space Station. So all candidates are required to study Russian.

Candidates also do a lot of reading during their training period. When they're not studying another language, they're probably reading manuals. These manuals explain how controls aboard the spacecraft will work.

To practice their skills, astronauts take tests inside something called a simulator. A simulator is like a really advanced video game. The candidate sits in a small room that looks exactly like a small room in a real spacecraft. The knobs, buttons, and screens all look identical. The simulator will create a fake situation that resembles a real situation that might happen in space. For example, the simulator will tell the trainee that a small fire has started in one of the spacecraft's engines. The trainee must use the simulator's computer and controls to put out the fire. Of course, the fire is not real, but the trainee gets to practice what he might have to do someday in a real emergency.

Even doing simple things in space like eating and sleeping can present its own challenges. One of the purposes of the International Space Station is to study the effects of living in space for long periods of time, so scientists know what to expect if they send astronauts on long trips to Mars—or beyond!

BECOMING AN ASTRONAUT

Finally, all astronauts must learn to fly. Even in orbit, a spacecraft moves around and must be pointed in the right direction. For some astronauts, being a pilot is their main job onboard the spacecraft. Those astronauts must fly fifteen hours each month during their training. Non-pilots must fly at least four hours per month. An astronaut never knows when he might be required to take control of the ship.

Challenges of Life in Space

Spending long periods of time in space is full of dangers for humans. Even a fully trained astronaut can find herself in trouble. Earlier we mentioned how hard it can be to adjust to loss of gravity. In space, astronauts hardly use their back and leg muscles at all. When they return to earth, they find it hard to walk and many get dizzy. To avoid that, astronauts use exercise equipment onboard their spacecraft. They push against giant rubber bands and do special exercises that don't require gravity. This keeps their bodies in shape.

Another concern for astronauts is radiation from the sun. Radiation is made of high-energy particles that are invisible. The sun emits millions of these particles, and they can be very harmful to humans. Usually the Earth's atmosphere protects us against radiation, but in space there is no such shield. Spacecraft are designed with tinted windows and special glass to keep radiation from getting through. But sometimes those shields aren't strong enough, and these invisible particles hit astronauts. Radiation can damage an astronaut's eyesight, in particular. Some astronauts have trouble seeing when they get back to Earth.

Astronauts also risk getting sick in space. If someone gets sick and can't be treated onboard, it can take weeks or months to get them back to Earth to see a doctor. Germs spread more quickly on a spacecraft because of the lack of gravity. The tiny germ particles don't settle onto surfaces. Instead, they float in the air and are breathed into human lungs. The rate of infection onboard a spacecraft is much higher than on Earth. For that reason, astronauts do their best to stay clean. Most spacecraft don't have showers, so astronauts take sponge baths. They use special soaps and shampoos that don't need to be rinsed off. These soaps work like hand sanitizer, evaporating after a few minutes.

When you're in space, obviously you can't just go outside for a quick walk. Being on board a spaceship for a long time can have many negative effects on your emotions.

And of course astronauts have to go to the bathroom when they're on a space missions! A normal flush toilet would not work in space because there's not enough gravity. Most toilets on Earth rely on gravity to pull the waste down. In space, a special toilet uses air to suck the waste back into a tank. The tank is emptied into space, but solid waste is stored onboard until the ship returns to Earth, where it's removed.

Preparing the Mind

Some of the biggest challenges of space are not to the body but to the mind. An astronaut spends long stretches of time in tiny, cramped rooms, with no contact with his loved ones back on Earth. He may get sick more than usual. It's difficult to sleep without gravity, so an astronaut is often tired too. These challenges are only increasing as astronauts spend longer periods of time in space. Astronauts on the International Space Station spend months at a time in space. They also live among many different cultures. An American must learn to understand a Russian and a Brazilian too.

Space programs recognize these challenges, and they prepare astronauts for them as best they can. Many space programs send astronauts to *isolation* chambers. In Russia, they put two astronauts in a room together for over a month. They can't see anyone else but each other. Many space programs are also teaching their astronauts about life in other cultures.

Astronauts also get support from back on Earth while they're on missions. "Care packages"

Getting Used to Zero Gravity

Scuba training is just one way astronauts prepare for the reduced gravity in space. Another way they train is in airplanes. The candidates are flown high into the sky, and then the plane takes a sharp dive. As the plane plummets toward Earth, candidates float up off the ground. They experience about 20 seconds of weightlessness! Then the plane corrects the fall and flattens out again, settling everyone back onto the plane's floor. The plane then climbs into the sky and repeats the dive again. Some astronauts complete up to forty falls a day.

Isolation is when something is all alone, separated from everything else.

NASA has successfully sent many unmanned spacecraft to explore Mars. Now, they think it might be time to send astronauts. A trip like this would take a very long time, and NASA wants to make sure humans could handle such a voyage.

are often sent to them. These packages carry little reminders of Earth—candies or hand-written letters from friends and family. In Russia, it is common to celebrate things in a big way. A Russian cosmonaut is likely to open all the gifts at once. But in America, the tradition is to open things slowly and take your time.

Being an astronaut takes a very special kind of person—and a lot of training!

Find Out Even More

One good way to do research is to use a bibliography. A bibliography is a list of books, articles, and other sources at the end of an article or a book. It lists all the sources that the author used when writing her piece. Once you've found a book or article that relates closely to your subject, you've found a great place to start, because chances are good that the bibliography will be full of more helpful sources!

Skim through the bibliography and write down any piece that sounds relevant to your research. Then go and find a few of those books or articles. Next check the bibliographies in *those* works for articles or books that might help you. By now, you should have a long list of books, probably more than you'll ever need. But remember that you probably won't be able to find many of the books on your list. You want to have enough.

Here's an important tip that will help you when you're skimming bibliographies to narrow down the sources that will be most useful to you: have a research question in mind. What question are you trying to answer with your research? Maybe your question is, "Exactly how do space toilets work?" As you search for more sources, keep that question in mind. Only choose books and articles that sound like they will help answer that question. It's easy to get distracted when you're doing research. You might be tempted to search for books about other features of spaceships. These books might be interesting but will they get you closer to answering your question? Stay focused by having a question in mind. You'll get a lot more done!

FOUR

The Future for Astronauts

R ight now the world is sending most of its astronauts to the International Space Station (ISS). Fifteen countries help run the station. Astronauts from many countries make trips up to it. For the past fifteen years, the space station has been the focus of space exploration. NASA designed ships, called "shuttles," that carried astronauts into space and back again. The shuttles dropped astronauts off at the space station as it orbited the Earth.

Setbacks

In 1986 and in 2003, NASA shuttles exploded, killing their crews. Americans realized that space travel is still very dangerous. Space travel is also very expensive. Governments don't always want to pay for new missions. U.S. politicians decided that Americans weren't as

The Orion spacecraft, which will look something like this, will be designed for much longer trips than the shuttles were used for. It will go to the moon, to asteroids, and maybe even to Mars!

interested in space travel and decided to cancel the shuttle program. Today, only Russia and China have space shuttle programs. NASA astronauts must travel aboard Russian rockets if they want to visit the ISS.

Many people are disappointed by the current trends in space travel. Since ending the shuttle program, NASA has focused more on unmanned missions to space. An "unmanned mission" usually means sending a robot or a satellite into space. Recently an unmanned mission sent the Curiosity robot to Mars. This little robot is taking photos and telling us a lot about "the Red Planet." But imagine how much more we could learn if a human was on Mars.

The good news for Americans is that manned space travel isn't gone forever. In fact, NASA is working on a new spaceship right now, called *Orion*.

Designing the Spaceship of the Future

Orion will be different from spaceships of the past. It is designed to go into deep space, beyond Earth or the moon. Someday *Orion* might take humans to Mars. *Orion* could take humans on trips that last as long as a year!

Orion will also be safer than all the space shuttles that came before it. Crews that fly inside *Orion* will have the choice to *abort* a flight after launch. Earlier crews didn't have that option. If something went wrong after launch, the crew couldn't fix the problem until the ship reached orbit. When returning to earth, *Orion* will use parachutes to float to the surface. The parachutes will work in any weather. Backup parachutes will fire if the main parachutes don't open correctly.

Orion can carry four astronauts at a time. Its first test flight is scheduled for 2014. It will launch 3,000 miles (4,800 km) into space and reach speeds of more than 20,000 miles (32,000 km) per hour. NASA has three places it plans for *Orion* to go: the moon, an asteroid, and Mars.

To **abort** something is to stop or cancel it.

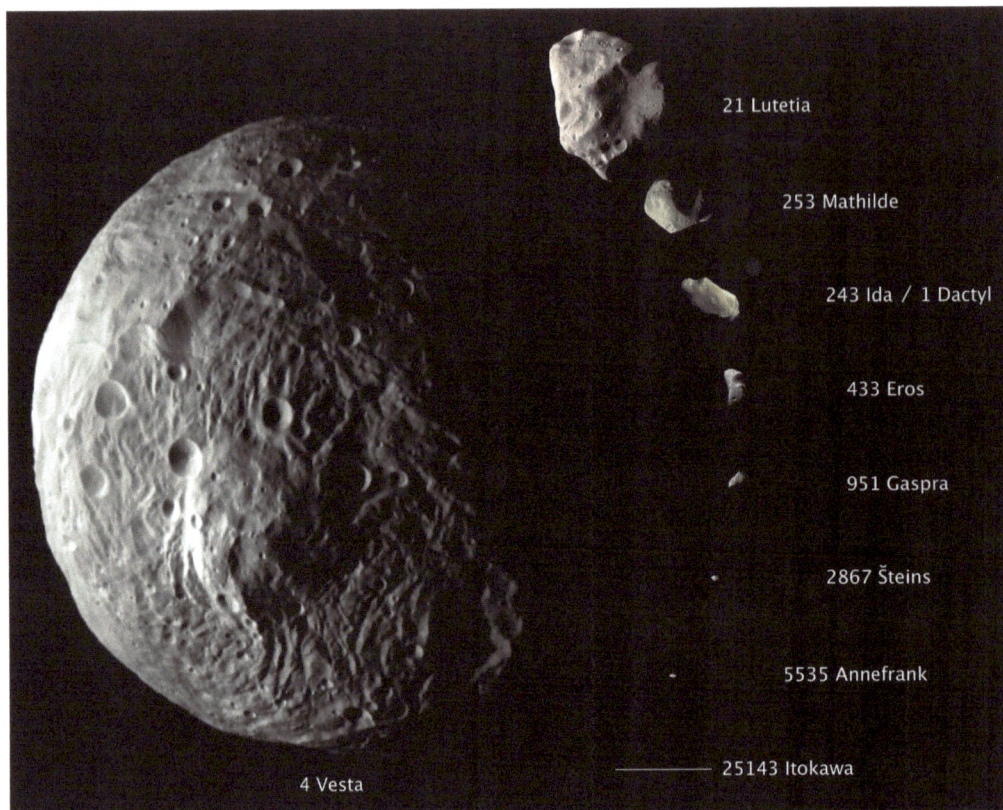

Asteroids can come in many shapes and sizes! Scientists have seen lots of them from far away, but we've never had a good chance to study one of those massive rocks up close.

Missions to the Moon

The moon continues to be a place of interest for space travel. The moon can tell us a lot about our own planet. The moon has been almost untouched by humans. By studying the moon we can learn a lot about the early years of our own planet. Think of the moon's surface almost as a museum, where millions of years of history are perfectly kept.

Missions to an Asteroid

Asteroids are rocks that are moving through space. They can be over a mile long or as small as a living-room sofa. Small chunks of rock enter the Earth's atmosphere all the time. Most of these tiny chunks, called meteors, burn up in our atmosphere. In fact, you've probably seen this happen when you look up at the sky and someone points out a "shooting star." That streak of light is really a tiny piece of rock burning up.

Small meteors are no problem for Earth's atmosphere. But a large asteroid could be a serious threat to human life. If it hit Earth, a large asteroid could send up a dust cloud that blocked out the sun and put us into a permanent winter.

Asteroids also carry secrets and clues that humans are interested in uncovering. Many asteroids come from far away, from exploded planets or distant stars. They might carry materials that we don't know about here on Earth. The raw materials found in asteroids could be used to build the space structures of the future. Or maybe they'll be used to make rocket fuels. We just don't know until we get access to a large asteroid.

For all these reasons, astronauts are training to land on an asteroid. NASA has plans for *Orion* to attach itself to an asteroid. Astronauts will take samples from its surface for scientific study. It will also prove that humans could stop an asteroid from hitting Earth. In the future, a dangerous asteroid could be "boarded" and redirected with rockets.

Missions to Mars

The robot missions of the past ten years have shown that Mars is a lot like Earth. It has a similar history, and probably had water at one point. Human explorers will look for more signs of life and find ways that humans might live on Mars someday. Astronauts who go to Mars will prove that humans can live for long periods of time on another planet. Many people believe that Mars is the best place for humans to live if anything bad ever happens to Earth.

Taking humans to Mars won't be easy. Mars is much farther from Earth than our moon. Right now, it would probably take around 200 days to get to Mars. That's 200 days to get there and 200 days to get back—over a year of space travel! That means a lot of fuel is needed. Carrying that amount of fuel will be difficult. We might need to find a new kind of engine before we can travel to Mars. Astronauts will need to carry a lot of oxygen and water with them too. The question is how to fit all that fuel, oxygen, and water into a small ship.

Radiation is also a big threat on Mars. NASA and other space programs will need to design special spacesuits to protect astronauts. They will design special materials to keep radiation from damaging the spaceship.

Astronauts from Around the World

More countries are sending astronauts to space every year. The United States and Russia still lead the world in space flight, but Iran, Japan, South Korea, Israel, Mexico, and other nations have all sent humans to space. Each country has sent dozens of people to space. And as the United States slows down its space program, countries like India and China are catching up to America and Russia. China has even built its own space station. China put its first person in space in 2003. Since then, China's Shenzhou missions have sent many more Chinese citizens to space and back. In China, astronauts are like celebrities. When a rocket launches everyone gathers around the TV to watch.

As other countries catch up with the United States and Russia, who knows what could happen. In a hundred years, maybe all nations will have astronauts in space! Other nations' space programs might even hire American astronauts.

Private Companies and Space Travel

In the future, space travel will be available to anyone who can afford it. We call this "private" space travel because the government does not pay for it. Companies around the world are starting to build their own private rockets and spaceships. Right now the average price is about $200,000 to become an astronaut. But the high price hasn't stopped wealthy people. Many millionaires have already signed up for private spaceflights that are scheduled for the coming years.

Each company has a different plan for its customers. One company wants to send its customers to the moon. Another company just wants to send its customers into orbit around the Earth for a few minutes.

There are dozens of private space companies around the world. Lots of people want to experience space for themselves. They want to know what it feels like to be an astronaut. Who knows, maybe one day, companies will sell space travel like they sell soft drinks. You might see an advertisement of an astronaut drinking a Pepsi!

An Exciting Future

A big thing that space travel has proven is that human beings are capable of creating brand-new ideas that never existed on the Earth. As scientists and engineers encountered new problems in space, they came up with new solutions. They invented new materials and designed new structures that had never existed before. They'll keep on doing this as space travel continues.

So if you want to be an astronaut, you'll want to be part of all that. You'll be interested in discovering both new problems and new answers. And all that new information will end up being put to use back on Earth too.

When it comes to space travel, one thing is sure—the future will be an exciting time!

Find Out Even More

YouTube is a great place to learn. There are millions of videos with information on every subject. But just like any other place on the Internet, YouTube has its dangers. Here are a few tips that will help you make the most of your time on YouTube:

- Start with "YouTube Education." If you don't know what YouTube Education is, ask your teacher. This is a special part of YouTube made just for students. You'll have a much easier time if you're using YouTube Education. It only links to videos that help you learn. It also removes comments that are mean or unhelpful so you won't have to see those things. When you're doing research, it's easy to get distracted. Use YouTube Education and you won't find yourself watching videos of cats jumping into boxes!

- Make a playlist. On YouTube, you can drag videos onto a playlist at the bottom of your screen. This will save you time and help keep you focused on your subject. Drag any videos that look helpful to your playlist and they'll play back-to-back without stopping.

- Avoid videos that try to get you to buy a product or click a link. Remember, there are thousands of companies that use YouTube to sell something. Never click a link that appears on a YouTube video or in its description. A good YouTube video will give you all the information you need without making you go anywhere else.

- Find a trusted source! If you watch a video that gives you good information, look for more videos by that user. If you click the user's name, you'll be taken to her page where you can browse more of her videos.

Here's What We Recommend

If you want to learn more about astronauts and space exploration, here are some good websites and books to get you started!

Online

European Space Agency (ESA) - How to become an astronaut
www.esa.int/Our_Activities/Human_Spaceflight/Astronauts/How_
to_become_an_astronaut

HowStuffWorks - "How do I become an astronaut?"
science.howstuffworks.com/question534.htm

NASA
www.nasa.gov

USA Today - So you want to be an astronaut? Here's what it takes
www.usatoday.com/story/tech/2013/10/05/what-does-it-take-to-be-
come-an-astronaut/2924145

In Books

Ferguson Publishing. *Space Exploration (Discovering Careers for Your Future)*. New York: Ferguson Publishing, 2008.

Greve, Tom. *Thanks NASA! (Let's Explore Science)*. Vero Beach, Fla.: Rourke Publishing Group, 2012.

Halls, Kelly Milner. *Astronaut (Cool Careers)*. North Mankato, Minn.: Cherry Lake Publishing, 2009.

Royston, Angela. *Astronauts Working in Space (The Big Picture: People and Culture)*. North Mankato, Minn.: First Facts, 2010.

Stone, Tanya Lee. *Almost Astronauts: 13 Women Who Dared to Dream*. Somerville, Mass.: Candlewick Press, 2009.

Index

About the Author

The author of over a dozen educational books for middle and high school students, Zachary Chastain lives in Binghamton, New York.

Picture Credits

www.ingramcontent.com/pod-product-compliance
Lightning Source LLC
Chambersburg PA
CBHW042018080426

42735CB00002B/93